Praise the Lord for who He

_____

_____

_____

_____

_____

_____

_____

MW00879911

_____

_____

_____

_____

_____

_____

My Answered Prayers & Gratitude:

_____

_____

People to Pray for

_____

_____

_____

_____

_____

_____

_____

_____

_____

My Prayer Requests & Concerns:

_____

_____

_____

_____

_____

_____

_____

_____

_____

Praise the Lord for who He is first!   Today's Date: _____

_____

_____

_____

_____

_____

_____

_____

My Answered Prayers & Gratitude:

_____

_____

_____

_____

_____

_____

_____

My Prayer Requests & Concerns:

_____

_____

_____

_____

_____

_____

_____

_____

Personal Confessions

_____

_____

_____

_____

_____

_____

_____

People to Pray for

_____

_____

_____

_____

_____

_____

_____

Praise the Lord for who He is first!   Today's Date: _____

_____

_____

_____

_____

_____

_____

_____

Personal Confessions

_____

_____

_____

_____

_____

_____

_____

My Answered Prayers & Gratitude:

_____

_____

People to Pray for

_____

_____

_____

_____

_____

_____

_____

_____

_____

_____

_____

_____

My Prayer Requests & Concerns:

_____

_____

_____

_____

_____

_____

_____

_____

Praise the Lord for who He is first!   Today's Date: _____

_____

_____

_____

_____

_____

_____

_____

My Answered Prayers & Gratitude:

_____

_____

_____

_____

_____

_____

_____

Personal Confessions

_____

_____

_____

_____

_____

_____

_____

People to Pray for

_____

_____

_____

_____

_____

_____

_____

My Prayer Requests & Concerns:

_____

_____

_____

_____

_____

_____

_____

_____

Praise the Lord for who He is first!   Today's Date: _____

_____

_____

_____

_____

_____

_____

_____

My Answered Prayers & Gratitude:

_____

_____

_____

_____

_____

_____

_____

My Prayer Requests & Concerns:

_____

_____

_____

_____

_____

_____

_____

_____

Personal Confessions

_____

_____

_____

_____

_____

_____

_____

People to Pray for

_____

_____

_____

_____

_____

_____

_____

Praise the Lord for who He is first!   Today's Date: _____

_____

_____

_____

_____

_____

_____

_____

My Answered Prayers & Gratitude:

_____

_____

_____

_____

_____

_____

_____

My Prayer Requests & Concerns:

_____

_____

_____

_____

_____

_____

_____

_____

Personal Confessions

_____

_____

_____

_____

_____

_____

_____

People to Pray for

_____

_____

_____

_____

_____

_____

_____

Praise the Lord for who He is first!   Today's Date: _____

_____

_____

_____

_____

_____

_____

My Answered Prayers & Gratitude:

_____

_____

_____

_____

_____

_____

My Prayer Requests & Concerns:

Personal Confessions

_____

_____

_____

_____

_____

_____

People to Pray for

_____

_____

_____

_____

_____

_____

_____

_____

_____

_____

_____

_____

_____

_____

Praise the Lord for who He is first!   Today's Date: _____

_____

_____

_____

_____

_____

_____

_____

Personal Confessions

_____

_____

_____

_____

_____

_____

_____

My Answered Prayers & Gratitude:

_____

_____

_____

_____

_____

_____

_____

People to Pray for

_____

_____

_____

_____

_____

_____

_____

My Prayer Requests & Concerns:

_____

_____

_____

_____

_____

_____

_____

Praise the Lord for who He is first!   Today's Date: _____

_____

_____

_____

_____

_____

_____

My Answered Prayers & Gratitude:

_____

_____

_____

_____

_____

_____

My Prayer Requests & Concerns:

Personal Confessions

_____

_____

_____

_____

_____

_____

_____

People to Pray for

_____

_____

_____

_____

_____

_____

_____

_____

_____

_____

_____

_____

_____

_____

_____

Praise the Lord for who He is first!   Today's Date: _____

_____

_____

_____

_____

_____

_____

_____

My Answered Prayers & Gratitude:

_____

_____

_____

_____

_____

_____

_____

My Prayer Requests & Concerns:

_____

_____

_____

_____

_____

_____

_____

Personal Confessions

_____

_____

_____

_____

_____

_____

People to Pray for

_____

_____

_____

_____

_____

_____

_____

Praise the Lord for who He is first!   Today's Date: _____

_____

_____

_____

_____

_____

_____

_____

My Answered Prayers & Gratitude:

_____

_____

_____

_____

_____

_____

_____

My Prayer Requests & Concerns:

Personal Confessions

_____

_____

_____

_____

_____

_____

_____

People to Pray for

_____

_____

_____

_____

_____

_____

_____

_____

_____

_____

_____

_____

_____

_____

_____

Praise the Lord for who He is first!   Today's Date: _____

_____

_____

_____

_____

_____

_____

_____

Personal Confessions

_____

_____

_____

_____

_____

_____

_____

My Answered Prayers & Gratitude:

People to Pray for

_____

_____

_____

_____

_____

_____

_____

_____

_____

_____

_____

_____

_____

_____

My Prayer Requests & Concerns:

_____

_____

_____

_____

_____

_____

_____

_____

Praise the Lord for who He is first!   Today's Date: _____

_____

_____

_____

_____

_____

_____

_____

My Answered Prayers & Gratitude:

_____

_____

_____

_____

_____

_____

My Prayer Requests & Concerns:

Personal Confessions

_____

_____

_____

_____

_____

_____

_____

People to Pray for

_____

_____

_____

_____

_____

_____

_____

_____

_____

_____

_____

_____

_____

_____

Praise the Lord for who He is first!   Today's Date: _____

_____

_____

_____

_____

_____

_____

_____

My Answered Prayers & Gratitude:

_____

_____

_____

_____

_____

_____

_____

My Prayer Requests & Concerns:

_____

_____

_____

_____

_____

_____

_____

_____

Personal Confessions

_____

_____

_____

_____

_____

_____

_____

People to Pray for

_____

_____

_____

_____

_____

_____

_____

Praise the Lord for who He is first!   Today's Date: _____

_____

_____

_____

_____

_____

_____

_____

My Answered Prayers & Gratitude:

_____

_____

_____

_____

_____

_____

_____

My Prayer Requests & Concerns:

_____

_____

_____

_____

_____

_____

_____

_____

Personal Confessions

_____

_____

_____

_____

_____

_____

_____

People to Pray for

_____

_____

_____

_____

_____

_____

_____

Praise the Lord for who He is first!   Today's Date: _____

_____

_____

_____

_____

_____

_____

_____

My Answered Prayers & Gratitude:

_____

_____

_____

_____

_____

_____

My Prayer Requests & Concerns:

Personal Confessions

_____

_____

_____

_____

_____

_____

_____

People to Pray for

_____

_____

_____

_____

_____

_____

_____

_____

_____

_____

_____

_____

_____

_____

_____

Praise the Lord for who He is first!   Today's Date: _____

_____

_____

_____

_____

_____

_____

_____

My Answered Prayers & Gratitude:

_____

_____

_____

_____

_____

_____

My Prayer Requests & Concerns:

_____

_____

_____

_____

_____

_____

_____

_____

Personal Confessions

_____

_____

_____

_____

_____

_____

_____

People to Pray for

_____

_____

_____

_____

_____

_____

_____

Praise the Lord for who He is first! Today's Date: _____

_____

_____

_____

_____

_____

_____

_____

My Answered Prayers & Gratitude:

_____

_____

_____

_____

_____

_____

_____

My Prayer Requests & Concerns:

_____

_____

_____

_____

_____

_____

_____

_____

Personal Confessions

_____

_____

_____

_____

_____

_____

_____

People to Pray for

_____

_____

_____

_____

_____

_____

_____

Praise the Lord for who He is first!   Today's Date: _____

_____
_____
_____
_____
_____
_____

My Answered Prayers & Gratitude:

_____
_____
_____
_____
_____
_____

My Prayer Requests & Concerns:

_____
_____
_____
_____
_____
_____
_____

Personal Confessions

_____
_____
_____
_____
_____
_____
_____

People to Pray for

_____
_____
_____
_____
_____
_____
_____

19

Praise the Lord for who He is first!   Today's Date: _____

_____

_____

_____

_____

_____

_____

_____

Personal Confessions

_____

_____

_____

_____

_____

_____

_____

My Answered Prayers & Gratitude:

_____

_____

_____

_____

_____

_____

_____

People to Pray for

_____

_____

_____

_____

_____

_____

My Prayer Requests & Concerns:

_____

_____

_____

_____

_____

_____

_____

_____

Praise the Lord for who He is first!   Today's Date: _____

_____

_____

_____

_____

_____

_____

_____

Personal Confessions

_____

_____

_____

_____

_____

_____

_____

My Answered Prayers & Gratitude:

_____

_____

_____

_____

_____

_____

_____

People to Pray for

_____

_____

_____

_____

_____

_____

_____

My Prayer Requests & Concerns:

_____

_____

_____

_____

_____

_____

_____

_____

Praise the Lord for who He is first!   Today's Date: _____

_____

_____

_____

_____

_____

_____

_____

My Answered Prayers & Gratitude:

_____

_____

_____

_____

_____

_____

_____

My Prayer Requests & Concerns:

_____

_____

_____

_____

_____

_____

_____

Personal Confessions

_____

_____

_____

_____

_____

_____

_____

People to Pray for

_____

_____

_____

_____

_____

_____

_____

Praise the Lord for who He is first!   Today's Date: _____

_____

_____

_____

_____

_____

_____

_____

Personal Confessions

_____

_____

_____

_____

_____

_____

_____

My Answered Prayers & Gratitude:

_____

_____

_____

_____

_____

_____

_____

People to Pray for

_____

_____

_____

_____

_____

_____

_____

My Prayer Requests & Concerns:

_____

_____

_____

_____

_____

_____

_____

_____

Praise the Lord for who He is first!   Today's Date: _____

_____

_____

_____

_____

_____

_____

Personal Confessions

_____

_____

_____

_____

_____

_____

_____

My Answered Prayers & Gratitude:

_____

_____

_____

_____

_____

_____

_____

People to Pray for

_____

_____

_____

_____

_____

_____

_____

My Prayer Requests & Concerns:

_____

_____

_____

_____

_____

_____

_____

Praise the Lord for who He is first!   Today's Date: _____

_____

_____

_____

_____

_____

_____

_____

My Answered Prayers & Gratitude:

_____

_____

_____

_____

_____

_____

My Prayer Requests & Concerns:

Personal Confessions

_____

_____

_____

_____

_____

_____

_____

People to Pray for

_____

_____

_____

_____

_____

_____

_____

_____

_____

_____

_____

_____

_____

_____

Praise the Lord for who He is first!   Today's Date: _____

_____

_____

_____

_____

_____

_____

_____

Personal Confessions

_____

_____

_____

_____

_____

_____

_____

My Answered Prayers & Gratitude:

_____

_____

_____

_____

_____

_____

_____

People to Pray for

_____

_____

_____

_____

_____

_____

_____

My Prayer Requests & Concerns:

_____

_____

_____

_____

_____

_____

_____

Praise the Lord for who He is first!   Today's Date: _____

_____

_____

_____

_____

_____

_____

_____

Personal Confessions

_____

_____

_____

_____

_____

_____

_____

My Answered Prayers & Gratitude:

_____

_____

_____

_____

_____

_____

_____

People to Pray for

_____

_____

_____

_____

_____

_____

_____

My Prayer Requests & Concerns:

_____

_____

_____

_____

_____

_____

_____

_____

Praise the Lord for who He is first!   Today's Date: _____

_____

_____

_____

_____

_____

_____

_____

My Answered Prayers & Gratitude:

_____

_____

_____

_____

_____

_____

_____

My Prayer Requests & Concerns:

_____

_____

_____

_____

_____

_____

_____

_____

Personal Confessions

_____

_____

_____

_____

_____

_____

_____

People to Pray for

_____

_____

_____

_____

_____

_____

_____

Praise the Lord for who He is first!   Today's Date: _____

_____

_____

_____

_____

_____

_____

_____

My Answered Prayers & Gratitude:

_____

_____

_____

_____

_____

_____

My Prayer Requests & Concerns:

_____

_____

_____

_____

_____

_____

_____

_____

Personal Confessions

_____

_____

_____

_____

_____

_____

_____

People to Pray for

_____

_____

_____

_____

_____

_____

_____

Praise the Lord for who He is first!   Today's Date: _____

_____

_____

_____

_____

_____

_____

_____

My Answered Prayers & Gratitude:

_____

_____

_____

_____

_____

_____

_____

My Prayer Requests & Concerns:

_____

_____

_____

_____

_____

_____

_____

Personal Confessions

_____

_____

_____

_____

_____

_____

_____

People to Pray for

_____

_____

_____

_____

_____

_____

_____

Praise the Lord for who He is first!   Today's Date: _____

_____
_____
_____
_____
_____
_____
_____

My Answered Prayers & Gratitude:

_____
_____
_____
_____
_____
_____
_____

My Prayer Requests & Concerns:

Personal Confessions

_____
_____
_____
_____
_____
_____
_____

People to Pray for

_____
_____
_____
_____
_____
_____
_____

_____
_____
_____
_____
_____
_____
_____
_____

Praise the Lord for who He is first!   Today's Date: _____

_____

_____

_____

_____

_____

_____

_____

Personal Confessions

_____

_____

_____

_____

_____

_____

My Answered Prayers & Gratitude:

_____

_____

_____

_____

_____

_____

People to Pray for

_____

_____

_____

_____

_____

_____

My Prayer Requests & Concerns:

_____

_____

_____

_____

_____

_____

_____

_____

Praise the Lord for who He is first!   Today's Date: _____

_____

_____

_____

_____

_____

_____

_____

Personal Confessions

_____

_____

_____

_____

_____

_____

_____

My Answered Prayers & Gratitude:

_____

People to Pray for

_____

_____

_____

_____

_____

_____

_____

_____

_____

_____

_____

_____

_____

My Prayer Requests & Concerns:

_____

_____

_____

_____

_____

_____

_____

_____

_____

Praise the Lord for who He is first!   Today's Date: _____

_____

_____

_____

_____

_____

_____

_____

Personal Confessions

_____

_____

_____

_____

_____

_____

_____

My Answered Prayers & Gratitude:

People to Pray for

_____

_____

_____

_____

_____

_____

_____

_____

_____

_____

_____

_____

_____

_____

My Prayer Requests & Concerns:

_____

_____

_____

_____

_____

_____

_____

Praise the Lord for who He is first!   Today's Date: _____

_____

_____

_____

_____

_____

_____

_____

Personal Confessions

_____

_____

_____

_____

_____

_____

_____

My Answered Prayers & Gratitude:

_____

_____

_____

_____

_____

_____

_____

People to Pray for

_____

_____

_____

_____

_____

_____

_____

_____

My Prayer Requests & Concerns:

_____

_____

_____

_____

_____

_____

_____

Praise the Lord for who He is first!   Today's Date: _____

_____

_____

_____

_____

_____

_____

_____

Personal Confessions

_____

_____

_____

_____

_____

_____

_____

My Answered Prayers & Gratitude:

_____

_____

_____

_____

_____

_____

_____

People to Pray for

_____

_____

_____

_____

_____

_____

_____

My Prayer Requests & Concerns:

_____

_____

_____

_____

_____

_____

_____

_____

Praise the Lord for who He is first!   Today's Date: _____

_____

_____

_____

_____

_____

_____

_____

Personal Confessions

_____

_____

_____

_____

_____

_____

My Answered Prayers & Gratitude:

_____

_____

_____

_____

_____

_____

People to Pray for

_____

_____

_____

_____

_____

_____

_____

My Prayer Requests & Concerns:

_____

_____

_____

_____

_____

_____

_____

Praise the Lord for who He is first!   Today's Date: _____

_____

_____

_____

_____

_____

_____

_____

My Answered Prayers & Gratitude:

_____

_____

_____

_____

_____

_____

_____

My Prayer Requests & Concerns:

Personal Confessions

_____

_____

_____

_____

_____

_____

_____

People to Pray for

_____

_____

_____

_____

_____

_____

_____

_____

_____

_____

_____

_____

_____

_____

_____

Praise the Lord for who He is first!   Today's Date: _____

_____

_____

_____

_____

_____

_____

_____

Personal Confessions

_____

_____

_____

_____

_____

_____

_____

My Answered Prayers & Gratitude:

_____

_____

_____

_____

_____

_____

_____

People to Pray for

_____

_____

_____

_____

_____

_____

_____

My Prayer Requests & Concerns:

_____

_____

_____

_____

_____

_____

_____

Praise the Lord for who He is first!   Today's Date: _____

_____

_____

_____

_____

_____

_____

_____

My Answered Prayers & Gratitude:

_____

_____

_____

_____

_____

_____

_____

My Prayer Requests & Concerns:

_____

_____

_____

_____

_____

_____

_____

Personal Confessions

_____

_____

_____

_____

_____

_____

_____

People to Pray for

_____

_____

_____

_____

_____

_____

_____

Praise the Lord for who He is first!   Today's Date: _____

_____

_____

_____

_____

_____

_____

_____

Personal Confessions

_____

_____

_____

_____

_____

_____

_____

My Answered Prayers & Gratitude:

_____

_____

_____

_____

_____

_____

People to Pray for

_____

_____

_____

_____

_____

_____

_____

_____

My Prayer Requests & Concerns:

_____

_____

_____

_____

_____

_____

_____

_____

Praise the Lord for who He is first!   Today's Date: _____

_____

_____

_____

_____

_____

_____

_____

Personal Confessions

_____

_____

_____

_____

_____

_____

_____

My Answered Prayers & Gratitude:

_____

_____

_____

_____

_____

_____

_____

People to Pray for

_____

_____

_____

_____

_____

_____

_____

My Prayer Requests & Concerns:

_____

_____

_____

_____

_____

_____

_____

_____

Praise the Lord for who He is first!   Today's Date: _____

_____

_____

_____

_____

_____

_____

_____

My Answered Prayers & Gratitude:

_____

_____

_____

_____

_____

_____

My Prayer Requests & Concerns:

Personal Confessions

_____

_____

_____

_____

_____

_____

_____

People to Pray for

_____

_____

_____

_____

_____

_____

_____

_____

_____

_____

_____

_____

_____

_____

_____

Praise the Lord for who He is first!   Today's Date: _____

_____

_____

_____

_____

_____

_____

_____

My Answered Prayers & Gratitude:

_____

_____

_____

_____

_____

_____

_____

My Prayer Requests & Concerns:

_____

_____

_____

_____

_____

_____

_____

Personal Confessions

_____

_____

_____

_____

_____

_____

_____

People to Pray for

_____

_____

_____

_____

_____

_____

_____

Praise the Lord for who He is first!   Today's Date: _____

_____

_____

_____

_____

_____

_____

_____

My Answered Prayers & Gratitude:

_____

_____

_____

_____

_____

_____

My Prayer Requests & Concerns:

Personal Confessions

_____

_____

_____

_____

_____

_____

_____

People to Pray for

_____

_____

_____

_____

_____

_____

_____

_____

_____

_____

_____

_____

_____

_____

_____

Praise the Lord for who He is first!   Today's Date: _____

_____

Personal Confessions

_____

_____

_____

_____

_____

_____

My Answered Prayers & Gratitude:

People to Pray for

_____

_____

_____

_____

_____

_____

My Prayer Requests & Concerns:

Praise the Lord for who He is first!   Today's Date: _____

_____

_____

_____

_____

_____

_____

_____

Personal Confessions

_____

_____

_____

_____

_____

_____

_____

My Answered Prayers & Gratitude:

_____

_____

_____

_____

_____

_____

People to Pray for

_____

_____

_____

_____

_____

_____

_____

My Prayer Requests & Concerns:

_____

_____

_____

_____

_____

_____

_____

_____

Praise the Lord for who He is first!   Today's Date: _____

_____

_____

_____

_____

_____

_____

_____

My Answered Prayers & Gratitude:

_____

_____

_____

_____

_____

_____

_____

My Prayer Requests & Concerns:

_____

_____

_____

_____

_____

_____

_____

Personal Confessions

_____

_____

_____

_____

_____

_____

_____

People to Pray for

_____

_____

_____

_____

_____

_____

_____

Praise the Lord for who He is first!   Today's Date: _____

_____

_____

_____

_____

_____

_____

_____

Personal Confessions

_____

_____

_____

_____

_____

_____

_____

My Answered Prayers & Gratitude:

_____

_____

_____

_____

_____

_____

People to Pray for

_____

_____

_____

_____

_____

_____

_____

My Prayer Requests & Concerns:

_____

_____

_____

_____

_____

_____

_____

_____

49

Praise the Lord for who He is first!   Today's Date: _____

_____

_____

_____

_____

_____

_____

_____

My Answered Prayers & Gratitude:

_____

_____

_____

_____

_____

_____

_____

My Prayer Requests & Concerns:

_____

_____

_____

_____

_____

_____

_____

Personal Confessions

_____

_____

_____

_____

_____

_____

_____

People to Pray for

_____

_____

_____

_____

_____

_____

_____

Praise the Lord for who He is first!   Today's Date: _____

_____
_____
_____
_____
_____
_____
_____

Personal Confessions

_____
_____
_____
_____
_____
_____
_____

My Answered Prayers & Gratitude:

_____
_____
_____
_____
_____
_____
_____

People to Pray for

_____
_____
_____
_____
_____
_____
_____

My Prayer Requests & Concerns:

_____
_____
_____
_____
_____
_____
_____

51

Praise the Lord for who He is first!   Today's Date: _____

_____

_____

_____

_____

_____

_____

_____

My Answered Prayers & Gratitude:

_____

_____

_____

_____

_____

_____

_____

My Prayer Requests & Concerns:

_____

_____

_____

_____

_____

_____

_____

Personal Confessions

_____

_____

_____

_____

_____

_____

_____

People to Pray for

_____

_____

_____

_____

_____

_____

_____

Praise the Lord for who He is first!   Today's Date: _____

_____

_____

_____

_____

_____

_____

_____

My Answered Prayers & Gratitude:

_____

_____

_____

_____

_____

_____

My Prayer Requests & Concerns:

_____

_____

_____

_____

_____

_____

_____

_____

Personal Confessions

_____

_____

_____

_____

_____

_____

_____

People to Pray for

_____

_____

_____

_____

_____

_____

_____

Praise the Lord for who He is first!   Today's Date: _____

_____

_____

_____

_____

_____

_____

_____

My Answered Prayers & Gratitude:

_____

_____

_____

_____

_____

_____

_____

My Prayer Requests & Concerns:

_____

_____

_____

_____

_____

_____

_____

_____

Personal Confessions

_____

_____

_____

_____

_____

_____

_____

People to Pray for

_____

_____

_____

_____

_____

_____

_____

Praise the Lord for who He is first!   Today's Date: _____

_____

_____

_____

_____

_____

_____

_____

Personal Confessions

_____

_____

_____

_____

_____

_____

_____

My Answered Prayers & Gratitude:

_____

_____

_____

_____

_____

_____

People to Pray for

_____

_____

_____

_____

_____

_____

_____

My Prayer Requests & Concerns:

_____

_____

_____

_____

_____

_____

_____

Praise the Lord for who He is first!   Today's Date: _____

_____

_____

_____

_____

_____

_____

_____

Personal Confessions

_____

_____

_____

_____

_____

_____

My Answered Prayers & Gratitude:

People to Pray for

_____

_____

_____

_____

_____

_____

_____

_____

_____

_____

_____

_____

_____

_____

My Prayer Requests & Concerns:

_____

_____

_____

_____

_____

_____

_____

raise the Lord for who He is first!   Today's Date: _____

_____

_____   ....

_____   : Personal Confessions :

_____   :   :
                                            :   _____ :
_____   :   :
                                            :   _____ :
_____   :   :
                                            :   _____ :
_____   :   :
                                            :   _____ :
                                            :   :
                                            :   _____ :
                                            :   :
My Answered Prayers & Gratitude: :   _____ :
                                            :   :
_____   :   :
                                            :   People to Pray for :
_____   :   :
                                            :   _____ :
_____   :   :
                                            :   _____ :
_____   :   :
                                            :   _____ :
_____   :   :
                                            :   _____ :
_____   :   :
                                            :   _____ :
_____   :   :
                                            :   _____ :
_____   :   :
                                            :   _____ :
My Prayer Requests & Concerns: ....

_____

_____

_____

_____

_____

_____

_____

_____

_____

Praise the Lord for who He is first!   Today's Date: _____

_____

_____   **Personal Confessions**

_____   _____

_____   _____

_____   _____

_____   _____

_____   _____

_____   _____

My Answered Prayers & Gratitude: _____

_____   **People to Pray for**

_____   _____

_____   _____

_____   _____

_____   _____

_____   _____

_____   _____

_____   _____

My Prayer Requests & Concerns:

_____

_____

_____

_____

_____

_____

_____

_____

Praise the Lord for who He is first!   Today's Date: _____

_____
_____
_____
_____
_____
_____
_____

Personal Confessions

_____
_____
_____
_____
_____
_____
_____

My Answered Prayers & Gratitude:

_____
_____
_____
_____
_____
_____
_____

People to Pray for

_____
_____
_____
_____
_____
_____
_____

My Prayer Requests & Concerns:

_____
_____
_____
_____
_____
_____
_____
_____

Praise the Lord for who He is first!   Today's Date: _____

_____

_____

_____

_____

_____

_____

_____

Personal Confessions

_____

_____

_____

_____

_____

_____

My Answered Prayers & Gratitude:

_____

_____

_____

_____

_____

_____

_____

People to Pray for

_____

_____

_____

_____

_____

_____

_____

My Prayer Requests & Concerns:

_____

_____

_____

_____

_____

_____

_____

_____

Praise the Lord for who He is first!   Today's Date: _____

_____

_____

_____

_____

_____

_____

_____

My Answered Prayers & Gratitude:

_____

_____

_____

_____

_____

_____

_____

Personal Confessions

_____

_____

_____

_____

_____

_____

People to Pray for

_____

_____

_____

_____

_____

_____

My Prayer Requests & Concerns:

_____

_____

_____

_____

_____

_____

_____

_____

Praise the Lord for who He is first!   Today's Date: _____

_____

_____

_____

_____

_____

_____

_____

Personal Confessions

_____

_____

_____

_____

_____

_____

_____

My Answered Prayers & Gratitude:

People to Pray for

_____

_____

_____

_____

_____

_____

_____

_____

_____

_____

_____

_____

_____

_____

My Prayer Requests & Concerns:

_____

_____

_____

_____

_____

_____

_____

_____

Praise the Lord for who He is first!   Today's Date: _____

_____
_____
_____
_____
_____
_____
_____

My Answered Prayers & Gratitude:

_____
_____
_____
_____
_____
_____
_____

Personal Confessions

_____
_____
_____
_____
_____
_____
_____

People to Pray for

_____
_____
_____
_____
_____
_____
_____

My Prayer Requests & Concerns:

_____
_____
_____
_____
_____
_____
_____
_____

Praise the Lord for who He is first!   Today's Date: _____

_____

_____   Personal Confessions

_____   _____

_____   _____

_____   _____

_____   _____

_____   _____

_____   _____

My Answered Prayers & Gratitude: _____

_____   People to Pray for

_____   _____

_____   _____

_____   _____

_____   _____

_____   _____

_____   _____

My Prayer Requests & Concerns: _____

_____

_____

_____

_____

_____

_____

_____

_____

Praise the Lord for who He is first!   Today's Date: _____

_____

_____

_____

_____

_____

_____

_____

Personal Confessions

_____

_____

_____

_____

_____

_____

_____

My Answered Prayers & Gratitude:

_____

_____

_____

_____

_____

_____

_____

People to Pray for

_____

_____

_____

_____

_____

_____

_____

My Prayer Requests & Concerns:

_____

_____

_____

_____

_____

_____

_____

_____

Praise the Lord for who He is first!   Today's Date: _____

_____

_____   Personal Confessions

_____   _____

_____   _____

_____   _____

_____   _____

_____   _____

_____   _____

_____

My Answered Prayers & Gratitude:

_____   People to Pray for

_____   _____

_____   _____

_____   _____

_____   _____

_____   _____

_____   _____

_____

My Prayer Requests & Concerns:

_____

_____

_____

_____

_____

_____

_____

Praise the Lord for who He is first!   Today's Date: _____

_____

_____

_____

_____

_____

_____

_____

My Answered Prayers & Gratitude:

_____

_____

_____

_____

_____

_____

My Prayer Requests & Concerns:

_____

_____

_____

_____

_____

_____

_____

_____

Personal Confessions

_____

_____

_____

_____

_____

_____

People to Pray for

_____

_____

_____

_____

_____

_____

_____

Praise the Lord for who He is first!   Today's Date: _____

_____

_____   **Personal Confessions**

_____   _____

_____   _____

_____   _____

_____   _____

_____   _____

                                        _____

My Answered Prayers & Gratitude:

                                        People to Pray for

_____

_____   _____

_____   _____

_____   _____

_____   _____

_____   _____

_____   _____

                                        _____

My Prayer Requests & Concerns:

_____

_____

_____

_____

_____

_____

_____

_____

raise the Lord for who He is first!   Today's Date: _____

_____

_____

_____

_____

_____

_____

_____

My Answered Prayers & Gratitude:

_____

_____

_____

_____

_____

_____

Personal Confessions

_____

_____

_____

_____

_____

_____

_____

People to Pray for

_____

_____

_____

_____

_____

_____

_____

My Prayer Requests & Concerns:

_____

_____

_____

_____

_____

_____

_____

_____

Praise the Lord for who He is first!   Today's Date: _____

_____

_____

_____   Personal Confessions

_____   _____

_____   _____

_____   _____

_____   _____

                                      _____

My Answered Prayers & Gratitude: _____

_____   People to Pray for

_____   _____

_____   _____

_____   _____

_____   _____

_____   _____

_____   _____

My Prayer Requests & Concerns: _____

_____

_____

_____

_____

_____

_____

_____

raise the Lord for who He is first!   Today's Date: _____

_____
_____
_____
_____
_____
_____
_____

My Answered Prayers & Gratitude:
_____
_____
_____
_____
_____
_____
_____

Personal Confessions
_____
_____
_____
_____
_____
_____
_____

People to Pray for
_____
_____
_____
_____
_____
_____
_____

My Prayer Requests & Concerns:

_____
_____
_____
_____
_____
_____
_____
_____

Praise the Lord for who He is first!   Today's Date: _____

_____

_____

_____

_____

_____

_____

_____

Personal Confessions

_____

_____

_____

_____

_____

_____

_____

My Answered Prayers & Gratitude:

_____

_____

_____

_____

_____

_____

People to Pray for

_____

_____

_____

_____

_____

_____

_____

My Prayer Requests & Concerns:

_____

_____

_____

_____

_____

_____

_____

_____

Praise the Lord for who He is first!   Today's Date: _____

_____

_____

_____

_____

_____

_____

_____

My Answered Prayers & Gratitude:

_____

_____

_____

_____

_____

_____

_____

My Prayer Requests & Concerns:

_____

_____

_____

_____

_____

_____

_____

_____

Personal Confessions

_____

_____

_____

_____

_____

_____

People to Pray for

_____

_____

_____

_____

_____

_____

Praise the Lord for who He is first!   Today's Date: _____

_____

_____

_____

_____

_____

_____

_____

Personal Confessions

_____

_____

_____

_____

_____

_____

_____

My Answered Prayers & Gratitude:

_____

_____

_____

_____

_____

_____

People to Pray for

_____

_____

_____

_____

_____

_____

_____

My Prayer Requests & Concerns:

_____

_____

_____

_____

_____

_____

_____

_____

Praise the Lord for who He is first!   Today's Date: _____

_____

_____

_____

_____

_____

_____

_____

My Answered Prayers & Gratitude:

_____

_____

_____

_____

_____

_____

My Prayer Requests & Concerns:

Personal Confessions

_____

_____

_____

_____

_____

_____

People to Pray for

_____

_____

_____

_____

_____

_____

_____

_____

_____

_____

_____

_____

_____

_____

Praise the Lord for who He is first!   Today's Date: _____

_____
_____
_____
_____
_____
_____
_____

Personal Confessions

_____
_____
_____
_____
_____
_____
_____

My Answered Prayers & Gratitude:

_____
_____
_____
_____
_____
_____
_____

People to Pray for

_____
_____
_____
_____
_____
_____
_____

My Prayer Requests & Concerns:

_____
_____
_____
_____
_____
_____
_____

raise the Lord for who He is first!   Today's Date: _____

_____

_____

_____

_____

_____

_____

_____

Personal Confessions

_____

_____

_____

_____

_____

_____

_____

My Answered Prayers & Gratitude:

People to Pray for

_____

_____

_____

_____

_____

_____

_____

_____

_____

_____

_____

_____

_____

My Prayer Requests & Concerns:

_____

_____

_____

_____

_____

_____

_____

Praise the Lord for who He is first!

Today's Date: _____

_____

_____

_____

_____

_____

_____

_____

Personal Confessions

_____

_____

_____

_____

_____

_____

_____

My Answered Prayers & Gratitude:

_____

_____

_____

_____

_____

_____

People to Pray for

_____

_____

_____

_____

_____

_____

_____

My Prayer Requests & Concerns:

_____

_____

_____

_____

_____

_____

_____

Praise the Lord for who He is first!   Today's Date: _____

_____
_____
_____
_____
_____
_____
_____

My Answered Prayers & Gratitude:

_____
_____
_____
_____
_____
_____
_____

My Prayer Requests & Concerns:

_____
_____
_____
_____
_____
_____
_____
_____

Personal Confessions

_____
_____
_____
_____
_____
_____
_____

People to Pray for

_____
_____
_____
_____
_____
_____
_____

Praise the Lord for who He is first!   Today's Date: _____

_____

_____   Personal Confessions

_____   _____

_____   _____

_____   _____

_____   _____

_____   _____

                                            _____

My Answered Prayers & Gratitude: _____

_____   People to Pray for

_____   _____

_____   _____

_____   _____

_____   _____

_____   _____

_____   _____

                                            _____

My Prayer Requests & Concerns:

_____

_____

_____

_____

_____

_____

_____

_____

Praise the Lord for who He is first!   Today's Date: _____

_____

_____

_____

_____

_____

_____

_____

My Answered Prayers & Gratitude:

_____

_____

_____

_____

_____

_____

_____

My Prayer Requests & Concerns:

Personal Confessions

_____

_____

_____

_____

_____

_____

_____

People to Pray for

_____

_____

_____

_____

_____

_____

_____

_____

_____

_____

_____

_____

_____

_____

_____

Praise the Lord for who He is first!   Today's Date: _____

_____

_____

_____

_____

_____

_____

_____

Personal Confessions

_____

_____

_____

_____

_____

_____

_____

My Answered Prayers & Gratitude:

_____

_____

_____

_____

_____

_____

_____

People to Pray for

_____

_____

_____

_____

_____

_____

_____

My Prayer Requests & Concerns:

_____

_____

_____

_____

_____

_____

_____

_____

Praise the Lord for who He is first!   Today's Date: _____

_____

_____

_____

_____

_____

_____

_____

My Answered Prayers & Gratitude:

_____

_____

_____

_____

_____

_____

My Prayer Requests & Concerns:

_____

_____

_____

_____

_____

_____

_____

_____

Personal Confessions

_____

_____

_____

_____

_____

People to Pray for

_____

_____

_____

_____

_____

_____

Praise the Lord for who He is first!   Today's Date: _____

_____
_____
_____
_____
_____
_____
_____

Personal Confessions

_____
_____
_____
_____
_____
_____
_____

My Answered Prayers & Gratitude:

_____
_____
_____
_____
_____
_____
_____

People to Pray for

_____
_____
_____
_____
_____
_____
_____

My Prayer Requests & Concerns:

_____
_____
_____
_____
_____
_____
_____
_____

Praise the Lord for who He is first!   Today's Date: _____

_____
_____
_____
_____
_____
_____
_____

My Answered Prayers & Gratitude:
_____
_____
_____
_____
_____
_____
_____

Personal Confessions
_____
_____
_____
_____
_____
_____
_____

People to Pray for
_____
_____
_____
_____
_____
_____
_____

My Prayer Requests & Concerns:

_____
_____
_____
_____
_____
_____
_____
_____

Praise the Lord for who He is first!   Today's Date: _____

_____

_____   **Personal Confessions**

_____   _____

_____   _____

_____   _____

_____   _____

_____   _____

                                          _____
My Answered Prayers & Gratitude:
                                          _____
_____
                                          People to Pray for
_____
                                          _____
_____
                                          _____
_____
                                          _____
_____
                                          _____
_____
                                          _____
_____
                                          _____

                                          _____
My Prayer Requests & Concerns:

_____

_____

_____

_____

_____

_____

_____

Praise the Lord for who He is first!   Today's Date: _____

_____

_____

_____

_____

_____

_____

_____

Personal Confessions

_____

_____

_____

_____

_____

_____

_____

My Answered Prayers & Gratitude:

_____

_____

_____

_____

_____

_____

_____

People to Pray for

_____

_____

_____

_____

_____

_____

_____

My Prayer Requests & Concerns:

_____

_____

_____

_____

_____

_____

_____

_____

Praise the Lord for who He is first!   Today's Date: _____

_____

_____

_____

_____

_____

_____

_____

Personal Confessions

_____

_____

_____

_____

_____

_____

_____

My Answered Prayers & Gratitude:

_____

People to Pray for

_____

_____

_____

_____

_____

_____

_____

_____

_____

_____

_____

_____

My Prayer Requests & Concerns:

_____

_____

_____

_____

_____

_____

_____

Praise the Lord for who He is first!   Today's Date: _____

_____
_____
_____
_____
_____
_____
_____

My Answered Prayers & Gratitude:

_____
_____
_____
_____
_____
_____
_____

Personal Confessions

_____
_____
_____
_____
_____
_____
_____

People to Pray for

_____
_____
_____
_____
_____
_____
_____

My Prayer Requests & Concerns:

_____
_____
_____
_____
_____
_____
_____
_____

Praise the Lord for who He is first!   Today's Date: _____

_____

_____

_____

_____

_____

_____

_____

Personal Confessions

_____

_____

_____

_____

_____

_____

_____

My Answered Prayers & Gratitude:

_____

_____

_____

_____

_____

_____

People to Pray for

_____

_____

_____

_____

_____

_____

_____

My Prayer Requests & Concerns:

_____

_____

_____

_____

_____

_____

_____

_____

Praise the Lord for who He is first!   Today's Date: _____

_____
_____
_____
_____
_____
_____
_____

My Answered Prayers & Gratitude:

_____
_____
_____
_____
_____
_____
_____

Personal Confessions

_____
_____
_____
_____
_____
_____
_____

People to Pray for

_____
_____
_____
_____
_____
_____
_____

My Prayer Requests & Concerns:

_____
_____
_____
_____
_____
_____
_____
_____

Praise the Lord for who He is first!   Today's Date: _____

_____

_____

_____

_____

_____

_____

_____

My Answered Prayers & Gratitude:

_____

_____

_____

_____

_____

_____

My Prayer Requests & Concerns:

Personal Confessions

_____

_____

_____

_____

_____

_____

_____

People to Pray for

_____

_____

_____

_____

_____

_____

_____

_____

_____

_____

_____

_____

_____

_____

_____

Praise the Lord for who He is first!   Today's Date: _____

_____

_____

_____

_____

_____

_____

_____

My Answered Prayers & Gratitude:

_____

_____

_____

_____

_____

_____

_____

My Prayer Requests & Concerns:

Personal Confessions

_____

_____

_____

_____

_____

_____

_____

People to Pray for

_____

_____

_____

_____

_____

_____

_____

_____

_____

_____

_____

_____

_____

_____

_____

Praise the Lord for who He is first!   Today's Date: _____

_____

_____

_____

_____

_____

_____

_____

Personal Confessions

_____

_____

_____

_____

_____

_____

_____

My Answered Prayers & Gratitude:

_____

_____

_____

_____

_____

_____

People to Pray for

_____

_____

_____

_____

_____

_____

_____

My Prayer Requests & Concerns:

_____

_____

_____

_____

_____

_____

_____

_____

Praise the Lord for who He is first!   Today's Date: _____

_____

_____

_____

_____

_____

_____

_____

My Answered Prayers & Gratitude:

_____

_____

_____

_____

_____

_____

My Prayer Requests & Concerns:

_____

_____

_____

_____

_____

_____

_____

_____

Personal Confessions

_____

_____

_____

_____

_____

_____

People to Pray for

_____

_____

_____

_____

_____

_____

_____

Praise the Lord for who He is first!   Today's Date: _____

_____

_____

_____   Personal Confessions

_____   _____

_____   _____

_____   _____

_____   _____

                                         _____

My Answered Prayers & Gratitude: _____

                                         _____
_____

_____   People to Pray for

_____   _____

_____   _____

_____   _____

_____   _____

                                         _____

My Prayer Requests & Concerns: _____

                                         _____

_____

_____

_____

_____

_____

_____

_____

_____

Praise the Lord for who He is first!   Today's Date: _____

_____

_____

_____

_____

_____

_____

_____

My Answered Prayers & Gratitude:

_____

_____

_____

_____

_____

_____

Personal Confessions

_____

_____

_____

_____

_____

_____

_____

People to Pray for

_____

_____

_____

_____

_____

_____

My Prayer Requests & Concerns:

_____

_____

_____

_____

_____

_____

_____

_____

Praise the Lord for who He is first! Today's Date: _____

_____

_____

_____

_____

_____

_____

_____

Personal Confessions

_____

_____

_____

_____

_____

_____

_____

My Answered Prayers & Gratitude:

_____

_____

_____

_____

_____

_____

People to Pray for

_____

_____

_____

_____

_____

_____

_____

My Prayer Requests & Concerns:

_____

_____

_____

_____

_____

_____

_____

_____

Praise the Lord for who He is first!   Today's Date: _____

_____

_____

_____

_____

_____

_____

My Answered Prayers & Gratitude:

_____

_____

_____

_____

_____

_____

_____

My Prayer Requests & Concerns:

Personal Confessions

_____

_____

_____

_____

_____

_____

_____

People to Pray for

_____

_____

_____

_____

_____

_____

_____

_____

_____

_____

_____

_____

_____

_____

_____

Praise the Lord for who He is first!   Today's Date: _____

_____
_____
_____
_____
_____
_____
_____

My Answered Prayers & Gratitude:

_____
_____
_____
_____
_____
_____
_____

My Prayer Requests & Concerns:

_____
_____
_____
_____
_____
_____
_____
_____

Personal Confessions

_____
_____
_____
_____
_____
_____
_____

People to Pray for

_____
_____
_____
_____
_____
_____
_____

Praise the Lord for who He is first!   Today's Date: _____

_____

_____

_____

_____

_____

_____

_____

My Answered Prayers & Gratitude:

_____

_____

_____

_____

_____

_____

_____

Personal Confessions

_____

_____

_____

_____

_____

_____

_____

People to Pray for

_____

_____

_____

_____

_____

_____

_____

My Prayer Requests & Concerns:

_____

_____

_____

_____

_____

_____

_____

_____

Praise the Lord for who He is first!   Today's Date: _____

_____

_____

_____

_____

_____

_____

_____

My Answered Prayers & Gratitude:

_____

_____

_____

_____

_____

_____

_____

My Prayer Requests & Concerns:

_____

_____

_____

_____

_____

_____

_____

_____

Personal Confessions

_____

_____

_____

_____

_____

_____

_____

People to Pray for

_____

_____

_____

_____

_____

_____

_____

Praise the Lord for who He is first!   Today's Date: _____

_____
_____
_____
_____
_____
_____
_____

Personal Confessions

_____
_____
_____
_____
_____
_____
_____

My Answered Prayers & Gratitude:

_____
_____
_____
_____
_____
_____
_____

People to Pray for

_____
_____
_____
_____
_____
_____
_____

My Prayer Requests & Concerns:

_____
_____
_____
_____
_____
_____
_____
_____

Praise the Lord for who He is first!   Today's Date: _____

_____   ....
_____   : **Personal Confessions**
_____   :
_____   : _____
_____   : _____
_____   : _____
_____   : _____
_____   : _____
                                          : _____
My Answered Prayers & Gratitude: : _____
                                          :
_____   : **People to Pray for**
_____   :
_____   : _____
_____   : _____
_____   : _____
_____   : _____
_____   : _____
                                          : _____
My Prayer Requests & Concerns: : _____
                                          ....

_____
_____
_____
_____
_____
_____
_____
_____

Praise the Lord for who He is first!　　Today's Date: _____

_____

_____

_____

_____

_____

_____

_____

My Answered Prayers & Gratitude:

_____

_____

_____

_____

_____

_____

_____

Personal Confessions

_____

_____

_____

_____

_____

_____

People to Pray for

_____

_____

_____

_____

_____

_____

My Prayer Requests & Concerns:

_____

_____

_____

_____

_____

_____

_____

Praise the Lord for who He is first!   Today's Date: _____

_____

_____

_____

_____

_____

_____

_____

Personal Confessions

_____

_____

_____

_____

_____

_____

_____

My Answered Prayers & Gratitude:

_____

_____

_____

_____

_____

_____

People to Pray for

_____

_____

_____

_____

_____

_____

_____

My Prayer Requests & Concerns:

_____

_____

_____

_____

_____

_____

_____

_____

Praise the Lord for who He is first!   Today's Date: _____

_____

_____

_____

_____

_____

_____

_____

Personal Confessions

_____

_____

_____

_____

_____

_____

_____

My Answered Prayers & Gratitude:

_____

_____

_____

_____

_____

_____

_____

People to Pray for

_____

_____

_____

_____

_____

_____

_____

My Prayer Requests & Concerns:

_____

_____

_____

_____

_____

_____

_____

_____

Praise the Lord for who He is first!   Today's Date: _____

_____
_____   Personal Confessions
_____   _____
_____   _____
_____   _____
_____   _____
_____   _____
_____   _____
                                          _____
My Answered Prayers & Gratitude:

_____   People to Pray for
_____   _____
_____   _____
_____   _____
_____   _____
_____   _____
_____   _____
                                          _____
My Prayer Requests & Concerns:

_____
_____
_____
_____
_____
_____
_____
_____

Praise the Lord for who He is first!   Today's Date: _____

_____

_____

_____

_____

_____

_____

_____

Personal Confessions

_____

_____

_____

_____

_____

_____

_____

My Answered Prayers & Gratitude:

_____

_____

_____

_____

_____

_____

_____

People to Pray for

_____

_____

_____

_____

_____

_____

_____

My Prayer Requests & Concerns:

_____

_____

_____

_____

_____

_____

_____

_____

_____

Praise the Lord for who He is first!   Today's Date: _____

_____

_____   **Personal Confessions**

_____   _____

_____   _____

_____   _____

_____   _____

_____   _____

_____   _____

                                          _____

My Answered Prayers & Gratitude:

                                          People to Pray for

_____

_____   _____

_____   _____

_____   _____

_____   _____

_____   _____

_____   _____

                                          _____

My Prayer Requests & Concerns: _____

_____

_____

_____

_____

_____

_____

_____

_____

Made in the USA
Monee, IL
27 September 2022

14789683R00065